PRO SPORTS
BIOGRAPHIES

BRYCE HARPER

by Elizabeth Raum

AMICUS HIGH INTEREST • AMICUS INK

Amicus High Interest and Amicus Ink are imprints of Amicus
P.O. Box 1329, Mankato, MN 56002
www.amicuspublishing.us

Library of Congress Cataloging-in-Publication Data
Names: Raum, Elizabeth, author.
Title: Bryce Harper / by Elizabeth Raum.
Description: Mankato, Minnesota : Amicus, 2018. | Series: Pro Sports
  Biographies | Includes index. | Audience: K to Grade 3.
Identifiers: LCCN 2016057216 (print) | LCCN 2016058338 (ebook) | ISBN
  9781681511351 (library binding) | ISBN 9781681521664 (pbk.) | ISBN
  9781681512259 (ebook)
Subjects: LCSH: Harper, Bryce, 1992---Juvenile literature. | Baseball
  players--United States--Biography--Juvenile literature. | Washington
  Nationals (Baseball team)--Biography--Juvenile literature.
Classification: LCC GV865.H268 R38 2018 (print) | LCC GV865.H268 (ebook)
  | DDC 796.357092 [b] --dc23
LC record available at https://lccn.loc.gov/2016057216

Photo Credits: John Green/Cal Sport Media/Alamy Stock Photo cover;
Jason Miller/Getty Images 2, 12–13; AP Photo/Alex Brandon 4–5 ; Robert
Beck/Sports Illustrated/Getty Images 6–7; Josh Holmberg/Icon SMI 259/
Josh Holmberg/Icon SMI/Newscom 8, 22; AP Photo/Rome News–Tribune,
Ryan Smith 10–11; Rob Carr/Getty Images 15;
John McDonnell/The Washington Post via
Getty Images 16–17; PR Newswire/AP 18–19;
 Chuck Myers/MCT/Alamy Live News 20–21

Editor: Wendy Dieker
Designer: Aubrey Harper
Photo Researcher: Holly Young

Printed in the United States of America

HC 10 9 8 7 6 5 4 3 2 1
PB 10 9 8 7 6 5 4 3 2 1

TABLE OF CONTENTS

HOME RUN HITTER

Bryce Harper is at bat. Smack! The ball soars into the stands. Home run! Harper plays for the Washington Nationals. He is one of the best home run hitters.

The Washington Nationals are also called the Nats.

RECORD BREAKER

Harper grew up in Nevada. He started playing t-ball at age three. He was a star baseball player in high school. He broke the school's home run records. He played as well as the **pros**.

At age 16, Harper was on the cover of *Sports Illustrated*.

COLLEGE BALL

Harper worked hard to finish high school early. He then went to the College of Southern Nevada. He played baseball there for one year.

GOING PRO

In 2010, Harper went pro. Harper got his start on the Nats' **minor league** teams. He played in the **MLB** fall league in Arizona. He hit 12 home runs in only 9 games. In spring, he played for the Hagerstown Suns.

THE NATS

Harper moved up to the major league in 2012. He's a great hitter for the Nats. He's also a good outfielder. He catches balls that come his way. That's an out!

Harper was voted the National League Rookie of the Year in 2012.

MR. ALL STAR

Not very many rookies get a spot on the All-Star team. But Harper did in 2012. He also made the team in 2013, 2015, and 2016.

In 2015, Harper was named the National League MVP.

KEEPING FIT

Harper works hard to stay fit. He lifts weights. He goes to batting cages. He eats healthy food. He sleeps 10 hours a night.

Harper says he eats a spoonful of ice cream at night. He likes mint chocolate chip best.

HARPER'S HEROES

Harper helps kids with cancer. He calls them Harper's Heroes. They come to the game. They watch him play. He takes photos with them. It's a fun day.

GRAND SLAM!

Harper hits home runs every season. In 2016, he hit his 100th home run. It was even a **grand slam**! Harper is a superstar!

JUST THE FACTS

Born: October 16, 1992

Hometown: Las Vegas, NV

College: College of Southern Nevada

Joined the pros: 2010

Position: Outfield

Stats: m.mlb.com/player/547180/bryce-harper

Accomplishments:

- National League Rookie of the Year: 2012

- All-Star Game appearances: 2012, 2013, 2015, 2016

- National League MVP: 2015

- *Baseball Digest* Player of the Year: 2015

- National League Season Home Run Leader: 2015, 42 home runs

- ESPY Award, Best MLB Player: 2016

WORDS TO KNOW

grand slam – a home run with three runners on base

minor league – baseball teams that are a level below the major league teams; players practice and develop skills before moving up to the major league team.

MLB – stands for Major League Baseball; the organization that makes the rules for professional baseball.

MVP – stands for Most Valuable Player; each year, the best player in the league wins the MVP award.

pro – a baseball player that earns money playing ball; it is short for professional.

rookie – a player in his or her first year on the team

LEARN MORE

Read More
Bodden, Valerie. *Bryce Harper*. Mankato, Minn.: Creative Education, 2014.

Goessling, Ben. *Washington Nationals*. Minneapolis: Abdo Publishing Company, 2015.

Websites
Harper's Heroes | Leukemia & Lymphoma Society
www.lls.org/harpersheroes

Official Washington Nationals Website | MLB.com
http://washington.nationals.mlb.com

INDEX